Teach the Children
The True Meaning of Easter

Written by
Jeanne W. Anderson

Illustrated By
Amy L. Hintze

*Happy Easter
to the Merrill Family

with love,
Jeanne W. Anderson
and
Amy L. Hintze*

Good Mountain Home Publishing

Published by
Good Mountain Home
Publishing Company

To order additional copies of this book email:
goodmountainhome@gmail.com

This book is dedicated to all of my wonderful friends who share my role
as Grammy, Grandma, Oma, MorMor, Nana, Draddy, Sugar or whatever your
unique name is for the special title of Grandmother.

My intent was to write the book in such a way that you are the
one telling this Easter story to your grandchildren.
ENJOY!

Teach the Children the True Meaning of Easter

"Grammy, today is the first day of spring!" the grandkids excitedly said as they ran in the front door of our home.

"I know! Did you see the beautiful daffodils growing by the sidewalk? Spring is my favorite time of year! Today is the day we decorate the house for Easter. Will you all help me?"

"Are we setting out the Easter Bunny decorations?"

"Yes, but first we must set out the very most important decoration. Let me reach up to the top shelf of the china cupboard, and I'll hand down this figurine. It's fragile so be careful."

"It's a statue of Jesus."

"Yes, it represents Jesus praying in the Garden of Gethsemane. Let's set it on the table in the front living room."

"That's where we put the little statue of Baby Jesus at Christmas."

"That's right! I know you all remember that Christmas is when we celebrate the birth of Jesus. Well, Easter is the time when we remember the atonement, crucifixion, and resurrection of Jesus."

"Those are big words. What do they all mean?"

As I sat down on the couch I said, "Let's take a break from decorating for a few minutes so that we can talk about the true meaning of Easter."

"I told you that this statue shows when Jesus was praying in the Garden of Gethsemane. He prayed to atone for our sins. This means that he took all of our sins upon himself. It was extremely sad and difficult for Him. He was in so much pain and agony that blood came out of the pores of His skin! His atonement made it possible for us to repent of our mistakes. This is the greatest gift that the people of the world have ever received."

"When Jesus had finished praying, very wicked men came into the garden with clubs and swords. They captured Jesus so that He would be crucified. His body was laid on a wooden cross, and his hands and feet were nailed to the cross. Jesus suffered on the cross for many hours until he died. This was the crucifixion. When we see a cross it reminds us that Jesus died for us. The cross is also a symbol of triumph over death."

"I saw a cross on top of the steeple at a church."

"Yes, many wonderful churches have a cross on top of their steeples. Other Christian churches like to put more focus on the Living Christ. With or without a cross though, the steeple on a church points to Heaven. If we are ever feeling sad or need help, the steeple will remind us to pray to Heavenly Father."

"Here's something interesting about the cross symbol: at Easter time, lots of people have a special tradition of baking and eating Hot Cross Buns on Good Friday. This is always the Friday before Easter Sunday. It is the day we remember the atonement and crucifixion of Jesus."

"But, Grammy, why is it called Good Friday? If it's the day that Jesus suffered and died, it should be called Bad Friday or Sad Friday."

I replied, "I know what you mean. I think it is called Good Friday because of all the good that came to the world. Jesus was willing to suffer and die for us so that we could be saved from our sins. This day had to happen so that we could receive the joy of eternal life!"

"So, what exactly is a Hot Cross Bun?"

"Oh, it's a yummy little round bun filled with raisins that is best eaten when it is still hot from the oven. It has a cross on the top of the bun cut into the dough or added on with frosting. Let's look for a recipe and try making some for Good Friday."

"What happened to Jesus next, Grammy?"

"The disciples of Jesus took his body off the cross and buried him in a tomb which was like a little cave in the side of a hill. They pushed a big rock in front of the tomb. The physical body of Jesus was in the tomb. When Jesus had died on the cross, his Spirit had left his body. On Sunday morning, the angels came from Heaven and moved the rock away from the tomb. A friend of Jesus, named Mary Magdalene came to the tomb. She saw that it was empty! She thought that someone had taken the body of Jesus. She was crying. The apostles of Jesus came to the tomb and also saw that it was empty. Then Jesus appeared to Mary Magdalene. Later, Jesus also showed himself to the apostles. At first they were all afraid because they knew Jesus had been killed. He had the apostles feel the prints of the nails in his hands and feet. Now, they knew that Jesus had been resurrected! This means that His spirit and His body had come together. Jesus was alive again! His resurrection was an absolute miracle!"

"So Easter is the time we remember the atonement, crucifixion, and resurrection of Jesus."

"That's right! Good job remembering those three big words!"

"Then why do we have the Easter Bunny?" asked the grandkids.

"That's a good question," I replied. "Hundreds of years ago in Europe, there was a legend of a young princess of spring time named Eostre . In English we say her name as Easter. It was believed that she ushered in the renewal of the earth after a long, cold winter. When the grass grows green, flowers bloom, and spring blossoms come out on the trees, the earth has come alive again. It's as if the earth has been resurrected like Jesus was resurrected."

I went on to explain, "Princess Easter had a magical pet bunny. He was known as Easter's bunny which over time he became known as The Easter Bunny. Some say that this magical bunny could lay colored eggs! Others believe that the eggs came from chickens and that the Easter Bunny changed the eggs into colored eggs."

"This bunny loved to play games so he would hide colored eggs the night before Easter for children to find. Sometimes, he also brings candy, books and little toys to put in the Easter Baskets for children who have been very good! Now, we have the fun of coloring the eggs ourselves and setting them out for the Easter Bunny to hide."

"Now that we understand so much more about Easter, let's put out the rest of the decorations. Here is a cute bunny wreath to hang on the front door, and here is a little Easter Bunny you can cuddle and play with. The bunny is also a symbol of new life. Lots of bunnies, baby chicks, ducks, lambs and all sorts of animals are all born in the spring. New Easter clothes are also a symbol of new life. Putting on the new clothes represents 'putting on a new you.' This means we will try to change our lives for the better. We will try to be more like Jesus."

"Now, I have another fragile decoration. It's my special sugar egg. Hold it carefully but look inside, and tell me what you see."

"Wow! I see a little lamb, bunnies, tiny flowers and trees, and little eggs!"

All of the grandkids took a turn looking inside the special egg while I explained, "Yes, the special signs of Easter are inside that egg. Easter Eggs are a symbol of Christ's resurrection from the tomb. When a new little chick emerges from the hard shell of the egg, it reminds us of Jesus emerging from the tomb."

"Sometimes children have races where they roll hard boiled, colored eggs on the grass. Rolling the egg represents the rock being rolled away from the tomb of Jesus."

"The eggs that are colored red are in remembrance of the blood that Jesus shed for us."

I continued to explain, "The little lamb inside that egg is also a symbol of Easter. Another name for Jesus is the Lamb of God. Do you remember reading in the Bible that people used to sacrifice lambs as a way to pay for their sins? This custom was to point people towards the perfect sacrifice of Christ on the cross. Jesus was Heavenly Father's perfect 'lamb' when he was sacrificed to pay for our sins."

"Here's our final decoration to set out. It's a beautiful flower called an Easter Lily. The white flowers symbolize purity and virtue. There is a tradition that lilies were found growing in the Garden of Gethsemane after Christ's agony. A beautiful white lily sprung up where each drop of Christ's blood fell to the ground in His final hours of sorrow and deep distress. So, Easter Lilies also commemorate the resurrection of Jesus Christ and our faith in everlasting life."

"Grammy, remind us what everlasting life means."

"It's a phrase that comes from the Bible. We should all memorize it."

"For God so loved the world that he gave his only begotten Son, that whosoever believeth in him should not perish, but have everlasting life." -John 3:16

"It means that we will live forever. Remember how sad it was when Great Grandma and Grandpa died? They will be resurrected like Jesus was. We will all be resurrected, and we will be able to live together with Heavenly Father and Jesus. That is the great story of Easter!"

"We have finished decorating now, but we have one final activity we need to do. Since you kids are sleeping over tonight, we have time to color some Easter eggs. Grandpa and I will get everything ready while all of you get your jammies on."

We set out the hard boiled eggs and the cups of colored egg dye on the table. While the kids colored eggs, we talked about how we could show appreciation to Heavenly Father and Jesus for the amazing gift of Easter. We decided we could always remember to choose the right, pray, read the scriptures, be kind and loving, and serve others the way Jesus did.

Little Luke, finished coloring the last egg in the carton.

He exclaimed, "Look at my egg, Grammy!"

I replied, "Oh, it's perfect! It's a red egg to help us remember...

The Sacrifice Of Jesus And The True Meaning Of Easter."

The Symbols Of Easter

Statue of Jesus: Represents Jesus praying in the Garden of Gethsemane to atone for our sins.

Church Steeple: Points to Heaven to direct our thoughts and prayers to Heavenly Father.

Cross: Reminds us of the crucifixion of Jesus who died for us and His triumph over death.

Princess Eostre: Legend of the Easter Princess who ushers spring time back to the earth. The earth is resurrected after the cold, dark winter.

Easter Bunny: Magical bunny who hides eggs and brings candy for the baskets of good children. The bunny also represents new life.

Egg: Represents the tomb of Jesus. When a chick emerges from the egg it represents Christ emerging from the tomb. Rolling Easter Eggs represents the rock being rolled away from the tomb.

Lamb: Represents that Jesus is the Lamb of God who made the perfect sacrifice for our sins.

Easter Lily: A beautiful white flower that grew in the Garden of Gethsemane. It represents purity, virtue, hope and everlasting life.

Hot Cross Buns: a sweet roll decorated with a cross, often eaten on Good Friday.

Good Friday: The day we remember the atonement and crucifixion of Christ and all of the good that came to the earth because of Jesus Christ.

Wearing new Easter Clothes: Represents "putting on a new you" to become more Christ-like.

Easter Sunday: The day we celebrate the resurrection of Jesus Christ and eternal life.

Tell Me the Easter Story

Tell me the Easter Story
Of Jesus, God's perfect son,
Who prayed in the Garden of Gethsemane,
Atonement for all, He won.

An Easter Lily was born
Where He bled from every pore.
On the cross, His flesh was torn.
The pain of our sins, He bore.

The Easter egg is a sign
Of His tomb on this earth.
His resurrection divine,
Spring is the time of rebirth.

Bunnies represent new life,
The church steeple reminds us to pray.
The Lamb of God was the sacrifice,
We remember Him this Easter Day!

-Jeanne W. Anderson

Easy to Make Hot Cross Buns

1 can refrigerated Crescent Dinner Rolls
1/3 Cup raisins
¼ tsp. grated orange peel
¼ Cup powdered sugar
½ tsp. milk

Heat the oven to 375 degrees. Unroll the dough and separate it into 8 triangles.

In a small bowl, mix the raisins and grated orange peel. Spoon about 1 tsp. of the raisin mixture onto the short side of each triangle. Gently wrap the corners of the dough over the raisin filling and roll to the opposite point; pinch to seal. Place the point side down on an ungreased cookie sheet.

Bake 10-12 minutes until golden brown. Remove the rolls from the cookie sheet onto a plate and let slightly cool.

In a small bowl, mix the powdered sugar and ½ tsp. milk until smooth. With a spoon, drizzle the icing into a cross shape on the top of each bun. If the frosting is too thick to drizzle, add another ¼ tsp. milk.

Serve warm. This recipe will make 8 buns. Dried cranberries could also be used instead of raisins.
This is a simplified recipe that children will have fun helping to make.

Enjoy!

Hot Cross Buns! Hot Cross Buns!
One a penny, two a penny,
Hot Cross Buns.
If you have no daughters,
Give them to your sons,
One a penny, two a penny,
Hot Cross Buns!

-Mother Goose Nursery Rhyme

Other Children's Books by Jeanne Anderson and Amy Hintze include:

Look Up (A true story of prayer and receiving inspiration)

The Story of Richard Ballantyne (Pioneer of the Sunday School in the Rocky Mountains)

A Cat that Quacks! (A story about talents, self-worth, and divine roles)

Teach the Children the True Meaning of Christmas (Santa teaches about Jesus and the symbols of Christmas)

To order any of these books, please contact Good Mountain Home Publishing at:

goodmountainhome@gmail.com

About the Storyteller

Jeanne and her husband, Steve, currently reside in Alpine, Utah. They are the parents of five boys; thus, they have served as Boy Scout Leaders for over 20 years. They also have five beautiful daughters that have married into the family. They have ten darling grandchildren! Jeanne has a Bachelor's Degree from Brigham Young University in Social Work. She loves gardening, all sports, being in the mountains, and writing stories for children. She is a 25 year volunteer with the Festival of Trees, a charity to help needy children at Primary Children's Hospital. If you would like to reach Jeanne or to order additional copies of this book, please contact her at goodmountainhome@gmail.com. She would love to hear from you!

About the Illustrator

Amy Hintze graduated from Brigham Young University with a Bachelor of Fine Arts degree in Illustration. In addition to drawing and painting for books and magazines, Amy is pursuing a degree in motherhood, with three adorable boys and two adorable girls. She has also enjoyed illustrating the Mormon Tabernacle Choir's Music and the Spoken Word broadcast since 2007. In her nonexistent spare time she enjoys being in the outdoors, listening to music, yoga , teaching art, and spending quality time with her wonderfully supportive husband, Brian. Amy met Jeanne when her small family moved to Alpine in 2000. Amy currently resides with her rambunctious family in Lindon, Utah. See more of her artwork at amyhintzeart.blogspot.com

Teach the Children
The True Meaning of Easter

It's spring time at Grammy's house! The grandchildren have come to help decorate for Easter and color eggs. This gives Grandma and Grandpa the chance to

"Teach the Children the True Meaning of Easter."

Most importantly, this book teaches of the atonement, crucifixion, and resurrection of Jesus. Grown-ups and children will also learn how Easter eggs, bunnies, and lambs all help to tell the Easter story of new life and eternal life. Storyteller Jeanne W. Anderson and artist Amy L. Hintze have teamed up to present this delightful illustrated story to share with your family for Easter.

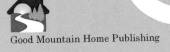
Good Mountain Home Publishing

Made in the USA
San Bernardino, CA
08 March 2015